Cutest Kittens Ever

QEB

Quarto is the authority on a wide range of topics.

Quarto educates, entertains and enriches the lives of
our readers—enthusiasts and lovers of hands-on living.

www.quartoknows.com

Copyright © QEB Publishing 2017

First published in the UK in 2017
by QED Publishing
Part of The Quarto Group
The Old Brewery, 6 Blundell Street
London, N7 9BH

Design: Melissa Alaverdy
Editor: Harriet Stone

A CIP record for this book is
available from the Library of Congress.

ISBN 978 1 68297 216 8

Printed in China

Contents

Which is the cutest of them all?
Read on and choose for yourself!

Abyssinian

With her big, pointed ears and alert eyes, an Abyssinian kitten looks super smart—and she is!

This beautiful cat is smart, curious, and will follow you around to see what you're doing. She also loves climbing up high, playing, and chasing things. This is a kitty who needs plenty of toys!

American Curl

If you're the proud owner of an American Curl kitten, you'll never be alone! This kitty loves being close to people, and will bump and nuzzle your face with hers to show how much she loves you.

She has soft fur and round eyes. Her name comes from her tufty, curled back ears.

American Shorthair

With her sweet, chubby face and silky fur, this kitten is totally adorable!

She's calm and quiet, making a great family pet. But she's not always quite as innocent as she looks—American Shorthairs LOVE to hunt, and are famous for catching mice. Many are silver tabbies, but they come in other colors, too.

American Wirehair

This kitten's fur is crimped and curly, giving her a springy, soft coat which is much like a baby lamb's wool. She's a bundle of fun who adores her humans and can't get enough cuddles and attention.

She's funny and loves to clown around, but if her owner is sad, she'll come and comfort them. Awwww!

Australian Mist

This adorable, chubby-faced kitten has silky soft fur, with scattered stripes or spots. She's a kind, gentle kitty who loves to lie in her owner's lap or roll around on the floor.

She's happy to be an indoor cat, as long as there are people around—especially children to play with!

Balinese

The Balinese is a long-haired, fluffy version of a Siamese, with the same beautiful blue eyes and colored "points"—the darker tips on their ears, nose, paws, and tail.

He loves people and will circle around your feet and "chat" to you nonstop. If you're his favorite person, he'll sit on you whenever he can, or even ride on your shoulder!

Bengal

The gorgeous Bengal is a sleek, spotted kitten with a wild side!

Bred from Asian jungle cats, he's happiest hunting, chasing, and climbing. He's super smart too—he'll figure out how light switches or door handles work, and play fetch like a dog. But he's also very loving and likes to follow his favorite human around.

Birman

Meet the Birman—a fabulously cute, loving, and snuggly-soft kitty with a big, bushy tail.

Birman kittens adore their human owners and are very curious. They've been known to get trapped in cupboards or cars because they'll jump in anywhere—keep an eye on this kitten!

Bombay

The stunningly beautiful Bombay was bred to look like a miniature black panther—and she does!

These kittens are born with blue or gray eyes, but they soon turn gold, contrasting with their amazing velvety black coats. Gentle and caring, a Bombay kitty will rub against your feet and meow politely to be allowed onto your lap.

21

British Shorthair

This cute and cuddly kitty is an ancient breed dating back to Roman times. His round face, big eyes, and thick, soft fur give him a sweet "teddy-bear" look.

A British Shorthair kitten loves to play and chase around, but he's also very affectionate. He'll even cuddle up to the family dog!

Burmese

Who could resist stroking and cuddling a velvety-soft Burmese kitty like this one? With his big, alert eyes, he's a curious, playful kitten who always wants to join in the fun.

He's funny, mischievous, and loves playing games with children. Just don't leave him on his own for too long—he'll get lonely and sulk!

Chartreux

This rare French breed of kitty is famous for her beautiful, thick, gray fur, which feels slightly woolly, like a sheep's.

At first, her eyes may be blue or green, but they soon become a stunning coppery-orange. A loyal, affectionate pet, she'll follow you from room to room and loves sitting on laps!

Chausie

The big-eared, long-legged Chausie is a mixture of a jungle cat and a pet cat—he's a little bit wild!

A Chausie kitten is a fearless explorer who loves to run, climb, and jump around nonstop. That doesn't leave much time for sitting on laps—but he'll still be loving and loyal to his favorite human.

Chinese Li Hua

This beautiful, golden-brown tabby kitten comes from China, and is also called the "Dragon Li".

He's very active and pounces on everything —Li Huas are famous mouse-catchers. But he's also a loyal, lovable kitty who'll do anything for his owner. One Chinese man even taught his Li Hua to fetch his newspaper!

Cornish Rex

This kitty may look odd, with her huge bat ears, tiny head, and long, skinny body—but her owners say she's adorable!

Her fur looks wiry, but feels incredibly soft. She's full of energy, running around and making amazing acrobatic leaps. She loves people, and will even sneak into her owner's bed to snuggle with them.

Egyptian Mau

This stunning, spotted kitty was first bred in ancient Egypt, and is named after the Egyptian word for cat—"Mau", of course!

She's a super-fast runner who loves stalking and pouncing. She prefers to be the family's only pet, and will "chat" to her owners with cute chirruping and squeaking sounds.

Havana Brown

Meet the rare Havana Brown, a beautiful dark chocolate brown kitten, sometimes almost black, with wise green eyes.

Nicknamed the "Brownie", she's a sweet, friendly kitty who's happiest when interacting with humans. If you're not giving her enough attention, she'll reach out and give you a poke with her paw!

Himalayan

A Himalayan kitten is a gorgeous, fluffy bundle, with thick, long fur and huge, expressive blue eyes. His slightly squished, grumpy-looking face is adorable!

He's a relaxed, gentle kitten who will play a little, but prefers to snuggle on a lap. Devoted to his owners, he likes lots of attention and cuddles.

Khao Manee

Unique, beautiful Khao Manee kittens are stunningly gorgeous. Their name is Thai for "white gem".

These white kitties, with sleek, velvety fur, can have blue eyes, golden-green eyes, or quite often, one of each color! They are incredibly friendly and curious cats, and prefer to be around humans all day long.

Korat

This gorgeous little kitten has stunning silvery-gray fur and a heart-shaped face. His big, intelligent eyes are blue at birth, then turn golden, and finally green.

42

In his native Thailand, he's known as the Good Luck Cat. He hates loud noises, but loves people—he'll climb on you, nuzzle you, and follow you everywhere!

Kurilian Bobtail

This kitty can be long-haired or short-haired, ginger, gray, creamy-white, or a mixture of colors. But all bobtails have a cute, short, stumpy little tail which gives them their name.

This kitten is a skilled hunter, and can even catch fish—but with humans, she's friendly, sweet, and gentle.

LaPerm

The LaPerm gets her name from her unusual wavy, curly fur. She's a ridiculously fluffy, scruffy kitty with the perfect "Who, me!?" innocent expression on her face.

She's cute, clever, and clownish. She gets into all kinds of mischief using her paws like hands to open doors, grab things, or bat you on the head!

Maine Coon

This tufty, fluffy kitten comes from New England, where Maine Coons used to be kept on board ships to catch rats.

Even as a kitten, a Maine Coon is big and strong. She's brave, a great swimmer, and loves water. Though shy with strangers, she adores her owners, and will play, chase, and clown around all day.

Manx

This funny, sweet kitten has a short, stumpy tail, or sometimes no tail at all! She sees herself as a "guard cat" and will often growl at strangers!

She's a friendly, fun-loving pet who's always snuggling up on or near her owners. Adventurous Manx kitties like exploring, splashing in water, and even going for car rides.

Nebelung

Just look at this kitten's adorable face and big, open eyes!
Nebelungs are a soft, silky breed with golden-green or blue eyes.

These quiet, gentle kitties can be shy with strangers. They take their time deciding who they'll trust to stroke and play with them. But once a Nebelung decides she loves you, she's loyal for life!

Norwegian Forest Cat

Norwegian Forest Cats are legendary in Norway, where they once caught mice for the Vikings and are featured in old fairy tales.

These cute, cuddly kittens have shaggy, woolly fur that's resistant to water and snow. They love playing, hunting, pouncing, and climbing—but they're also friendly and playful, with a very loud purr!

Ocicat

With her big ears and beautiful leopard spots, the Ocicat is named for her resemblance to the ocelot, a large wild cat.

She's very smart and can recognize her name, learn tricks, and figure out how to open cupboards. But this kitty isn't fierce at all—she's just a friendly, playful, energetic handful!

Orange Tabby

This kitten's stripy orange coat can also be described as marmalade or ginger. Several different breeds can have this color, but strangely, almost all orange tabbies are boys!

Owners of ginger kitties say they are easygoing, and love eating and lazing around. Their adorable pink noses are sometimes dotted with dark freckles. Super cute!

Persian

With his long fur, upturned nose, chubby cheeks, and huge eyes, a Persian kitten is the ultimate cuddly fluffball cutie-pie! He's gorgeous, and he knows it—Persians *love* to pose.

Though some have a slightly grumpy face, they are sweet, chilled-out cats who like snuggling up at home and interacting with their beloved owners.

Peterbald

This is what normal kittens would look like without their thick coats! Some Peterbalds have very short fur, while others are totally bald.

These kittens can look a bit strange, with their huge bat ears, pointy faces, and wrinkly skin—but they are still adorable! They are very smart, curious kittens with a super loud purr.

Pixie-bob

The handsome Pixie-bob was bred to look like a bobcat—a big stripy wild cat with a "bobbed" or stumpy tail.

He's not really wild, though—he's the ultimate sweet, lovable, and lively pet kitten. He can't wait to see you and jumps up to snuggle as soon as you sit down!

Ragamuffin

This fluffy, lovable, and huggable kitten is totally relaxed. She loves being picked up and played with by children—she's even happy to ride around in a toy baby stroller!

She's friendly with everyone, including other pets. When not busy being cuddled, she likes to laze around in the softest, snuggliest spots she can find.

Ragdoll

This gorgeous fluffy bundle has to be one of the cutest kittens ever! She's a large, very furry kitty with beautiful blue eyes.

Ragdolls got their name because they love being picked up and hugged, and are kind to children. They're also nicknamed "puppycats" because they're so loving and loyal.

Russian Blue

A Russian blue kitten is beautiful, but not actually blue! For cats, the word "blue" means slate gray. This sweet kitty has thick, soft fur and yellow-green eyes.

His mouth seems to smile, making him extra cute! Be gentle with him, though —he's a shy, sensitive little thing, who often hides from strangers.

Savannah

A Savannah kitty is a real handful! Beautiful, big-eyed, and stripy, she's half pet cat and half serval, a wild cat from Africa.

She'll climb, explore, and jump anywhere. She can turn on faucets, open doors, and chew things just like a puppy. But she's also loyal and loving to her owner, and enjoys being stroked or cuddled.

Scottish Fold

With her folded-over ears, round face, and big, thoughtful eyes, a Scottish Fold has to be one of the cutest kittens there is!

Besides curling up on laps and playing with her favorite human, this kitten likes to laze and flop around in all kinds of silly poses. Adorable!

Selkirk Rex

This adorable kitty has a thick, curly coat that makes him look like a soft, huggable, cuddly toy. Everyone wants to stroke his unusual fur, and luckily he doesn't mind at all!

He's a patient, kind, and loving kitten with a sweet, gentle meow. He never gets tired of playing and interacting with people.

Siamese

Meeoooow! This smart, friendly kitten is famous for his endless meowing and yowling to get your attention, a cuddle, or some food.

Siamese are also known for their beautiful blue eyes and colored "points".

Siberian

Kittens don't come much cuter than the adorable Siberian! This roly-poly, cuddly fluffball has long, thick fur and beautiful eyes.

Active and playful, this kitten is a great climber and jumper. But most of all, he loves attention! He'll sit on your book or keyboard and chirp and purr at you to get the cuddles he wants.

Singapura

The Singapura is a teeny-tiny kitty, as this is one of the smallest of all cat breeds.

She's a very beautiful kitten with cream and pale brown fur, big ears, and huge, pale bluish-green eyes. She's curious and playful, and likes to be close to people, but shhh!—she hates loud noises.

Snowshoe

How sweet is this gorgeous kitten? The soft-furred, pretty Snowshoe gets her name from her feet, which are often pure white.

She loves to "talk" to her owner in meows, purrs, and chirps. In fact, she's so friendly and chatty, some people say she thinks she's a human!

Sokoke

Beautiful, brown, and stripy, the Sokoke is a rare forest cat from Kenya, Africa. Even as a kitten, he's alert, brave, and strong.

He doesn't really like laps, but he's friendly, caring, and chatty, and always meowing and purring. He *loves* visitors, and will always go to the door to see who's arrived!

Somali

This gorgeous, fluffy kitty often has a "mane" of thick fur around his neck. He's full of energy and loves going outdoors to explore, climb, and leap into the air.

He can be sassy and stubborn, but also likes to snuggle up to his owners. He especially enjoys playing with his favorite human's hair or beard!

Sphynx

This unusual kitten looks as bald as can be, but he actually has peachy-soft fuzz instead of longer fur.

He looks a bit like a cute alien with his wrinkly skin, long neck, and huge, wide-apart eyes. He's a bouncy, funny kitten who loves leaping around and climbing on his humans like a mischievous monkey.

Tonkinese

You'll never be bored with a Tonkinese kitten around! This excitable, creamy-white or gray-brown furball nicknamed the "Tonk", is mischievous, funny, and full of energy.

She'll bounce, roll, and race around the house and get into everything—then climb all over you wanting a stroke and a cuddle!

Turkish Van

This ancient breed from the mountains of Turkey has an amazingly soft, thick, and fluffy coat to keep her warm.

She's an action-packed, energetic kitten who's enthusiastic about everything whether it's playing, climbing, exploring, eating, or swimming (Turkish Vans love water)! She also has a strange meow that is a little like a sheep's "baa". Sweet!

Picture acknowledgments

Picture Credits
fc= front cover, bc=back cover, bg=background, t=top, b=bottom, l=left, r=right, c=center

AdobeStock: 28c coulanges

Alamy: 10c imageBROKER, 11tl Arco Images GmbH, 11tr Juniors Bildarchiv GmbH, 13tl Dorling Kindersley ltd, 13tr Dorling Kindersley ltd , 13br JAV Clix / Stockimo, 25b Juniors Bildarchiv GmbH, 31b Amy Lv, 37c Life on white, 39b LJ Wilson-Knight, 43br Tierfotoagentur, 45cl Tierfotoagentur, 47b Tierfotoagentur, 51tl Mark J. Barrett, 51cr imageBROKER, 51br blickwinkel, 59bl Mark J. Barrett, 62c Tierfotoagentur, 63tr Tierfotoagentur, 63b Tierfotoagentur, 64c petographer, 65c petographer, 67bl Juniors Bildarchiv GmbH, 73t Tierfotoagentur, 82c Petra Wegner, 83tr Petra Wegner

Ardea: 53r © Jean-Michel Labat

Dreamstime: 25tr © Lifeontheside, 30c © Li Cao, 31tl © Li Cao, 31tr © Li Cao, 53tl © Mouskie, 53b © Mouskie, 68c © Linncurrie

Getty: fc 101cats, 12c Tracy Morgan Animal Photography Dorling Kindersley, 27tl 101cats, 27tr 101cats, 27bl Manfred Rutz, 27br 101cats, 29c Satyendra Kumar Tiwari

FLPA: 2-3 bg Jeanette Hutfluss/Tierfotoagentur, 9tl Mitsuaki Iwago/Minden Pictures, 17t PICANI/Imagebroker, 17bl Angela Hampton, 18c Sabine Schwerdtfeger/Tierfotoagentur, 22c Jeanette Hutfluss/Tierfotoagentur, 34c PICANI/Imagebroker, 42c PICANI/Imagebroker, 43tl Chris Brignell, 43bl PICANI/Imagebroker, 49r ImageBroker/Imagebroker, 52c Imagebroker, 54c Ramona Richter/Tierfotoagentur, 55t Ramona Richter/Tierfotoagentur, 55br IMAGEBROKER,ERICH SCHMIDT/Imagebroker, 56c Ramona Richter/ Tierfotoagentur, 57tl Ramona Richter/Tierfotoagentur, 57tr Blue Valentines/Imagebroker, 57bl Ramona Richter/ Tierfotoagentur, 57br Blue Valentines/Imagebroker, 61tr Mitsuaki Iwago, 69t Ramona Richter/ Tierfotoagentur, 73cl Annette Mirsberger/Tierfotoagentur, 73br Sabine Schwerdtfeger/Tierfotoagentur, 77tl Ramona Richter/Tierfotoagentur, 80c Ramona Richter/Tierfotoagentur, 81t Ramona Richter/Tierfotoagentur, 81bl Ramona Richter/Tierfotoagentur, 81br Ramona Richter/Tierfotoagentur, 83l Ramona Richter/Tierfotoagentur, 83br Ramona Richter/Tierfotoagentur, 86c J.-L. Klein and M.-L. Hubert, 87c J.-L. Klein and M.-L. Hubert, 90c IMAGEBROKER,ERICH SCHMIDT/Imagebroker, 91bl Chris Brignell, 91br Chris Brignell, 93tr Chris Brignell, 93br Ramona Richter/Tierfotoagentur

istock: 58c 101cats, 59tl Okssi68, 59tr lopurice, 59br ntzolov

Nature picture Library: 94c © Jane Burton, 95tl © Jane Burton, 95bl © Jane Burton

Shutterstock: bc Linn Currie, 1c Linn Currie, 4c Seregraff, 4tr Seregraff, 5b Nataliya Kuznetsova, 5tl Denys Dolnikov, 6c Robynrg, 7tl Vasiliy Khimenko, 7tr Eric Isselee, 7bl Eric Isselee, 7br Linn Currie, 8c Damona, 9tr Tony Campbell, 9b Top Photo Engineer, 11b rolehcab, 14c SUSAN LEGGETT, 15tl Kucher Serhii, 15tr BravissimoS, 15bl Cedric Crucke, 15br Jaren Jai Wicklund, 16c Utekhina Anna, 17cl Utekhina Anna, 17br Seregraff, 19tl Borkin Vadim, 19tr Juhku, 19bl Borkin Vadim, 19br Eric Isselee, 20c Patchaya Safari, 21tl Andrey Kuzmichev, 21tr Ed-Ni Photo, 21bl dien, 21br Eric Isselee, 23tl Chendongshan, 23tr Utekhina Anna, 23b Chendongshan, 24c Adya, 25tl Jagodka, 26c Gosha Georgiev, 32c Imageman, 33tl Oleg Kozlov, 33tr RomanSo, 33b Eugeniya Ardysheva, 35tl ARTSILENSE, 35b Krissi Lundgren, 35tr kuban_girl, 36c Eric Isselee, 38c Linn Currie, 39tl Stephen Orsillo, 39tr Zina Seletskaya, 40c Lizmyosotis, 41tl Kraipet Sritong, 41bl NaNae, 41r Bruno Passigatti, 43tr Cyril PAPOT, 44c TalyaPhoto, 45tr Vagengeim, 45bl ingret, 45br TalyaPhoto, 46c Linn Currie, 47tl Linn Currie, 47tr Linn Currie, 48c TalyaPhoto, 49tl Linn Currie, 49bl Artem Kursin, 50c Lisa Charbonneau, 51tr Cindi Wilson, 51bl Cindi Wilson, 55bl Krissi Lundgren, 60c Eric Isselee, 61tl Vasiliy Koval, 61bl ANURAK PONGPATIMET, 61br Gelpi, 63tl Toloubaev Stanislav, 66c Alex Papp, 67t Dmitriy Kostylev, 67br Tatiana Makotra, 69br dezi, 69bl Linn Currie, 70c Gita Kulinitch Studio, 71t Petr Jilek, 71tr Review News, 71bl Utekhina Anna, 71br Kamil Martinovsky, 72c Lindasj22, 73bl Lindasj22, 74c Medvedev Andrey, 75tl ADA_photo, 75tr Volodymyr Burdiak, 75bl Medvedev Andrey, 75br Cherry-Merry, 76c Ludmila Pankova, 77tr kuban_girl, 77b Utekhina Anna, 78c dedek, 79tl Chepko Danil Vitalevich, 79br nrey, 79tr Dora Zett, 79bl Inga Gedrovicha, 84c EVasilieva, 85tl EVasilieva, 85tr Stephen Mcsweeny, 85b Brenda Carson, 88c Sarah Newton, 89t nelik, 89cl nelik, 89bl Nataliya Kuznetsova, 89br Lapina, 91t ANCH, 92c dezi, 93tl dezi, 93bl dezi, 95r Linn Currie, 96bg Jagodka